DISCOVERING ARCHAEOLOGY

A GUIDE FOR BEGINNERS

DISCOVERING ARCHAEOLOGY

A GUIDE FOR BEGINNERS

"Success is in the pages of this book –
Unlock your potential!"

ROSHNI DAHAL

For

My parents, who teach me.

My mentor, who guides me.

My curiosity, who inspires me.

Preface

In this book, Discovering Archaeology: A Guide for Beginners, I will show you the amazing world of archaeology. Archaeology is the study of the past through the examination of artifacts and other physical remains. It is an amazing field that is full of discovery and exploration, and I believe that anyone can become an archaeologist with the right knowledge and guidance.

In this book, I will provide you with the basics of archaeology and the necessary tools to begin your journey. I will introduce you to the many types of archaeology, the methods of excavation and analysis. You will learn how to read and interpret artifacts, how to use technology to help you in your research.

I will also discuss the importance of preserving archaeological sites. I will explain how to ensure that their discoveries are shared with the world.

I hope that this book will be a helpful guide for anyone interested in archaeology.

Lucknow
January 2023

Roshni Dahal

Editor

Nikhil Kr. Vishwakarma

Contents

INTRODUCTION

Archaeology is the scientific study of past human cultures and societies, through the recovery, analysis and interpretation of material remains, such as artefacts, architecture, and ecofacts. Archaeology is a broad field that encompasses many different methods and sub-disciplines, including bioarchaeology, historical archaeology, and classical archaeology. Archaeology is a science that uses the material remains of the past to gain insight into the behaviour and lifeways of ancient peoples.

 The term "archaeology" was first coined in the late 19th century by the British antiquarian John Lubbock in his work Pre-Historic Times, as an attempt to distinguish between what was then known as "antiquarianism" and the newly emerging science of archaeology. The term is derived from the Greek arkhaios, meaning "ancient", and logia, meaning "study."

Archaeological methods and techniques are used to study the material remains of past cultures, such as material artifacts, ecofacts, and features. Archaeologists employ a variety of techniques to excavate, analyze, and interpret artifacts, such as radiocarbon dating, stratigraphic excavation, and the study of artifact types.

Archaeology has contributed greatly to our knowledge of past societies, and has helped to answer many questions about the development of human cultures across the world. By studying the material remains of past societies, archaeologists can gain insight into the life and culture of the people who created them, as well as the environment in which they lived. Archaeology is an invaluable tool for understanding both the past and the present, and its findings are often used to inform modern policy and planning decisions.

ORIGIN OF ARCHAEOLOGY

Archaeology is the study of the past through material remains such as artifacts, architecture, and culture. It is an interdisciplinary field that draws on the expertise of the humanities and sciences in order to understand the past.

The origin of archaeology can be traced back to ancient Greece. In the 5th century BCE, *Herodotus, a Greek historian*, was the first to record observations about ancient sites, such as Troy and Egypt, in his writings. He documented the ruins of past civilizations and took an interest in their artifacts.

In the 17th century, the antiquarianism movement began in Europe. This movement encouraged the study of antiquities and the documentation of ancient sites. During this period, many of the first archaeological discoveries were made. In 1666, the *English antiquarian John Aubrey* documented Stonehenge and in 1741, the *French adventurer Antoine-Simon Le Page du Pratz* discovered the remains of the Natchez Indian mounds in Louisiana.

In the 19th century, the science of archaeology was established. The first archaeological excavations were carried out by the *French scholar, Jacques Boucher de Perthes in the 1840s*. He unearthed artifacts that were evidence of an ancient civilization. In the 1860s, the *British archaeologist, Augustus Pitt-Rivers*, developed the technique of stratigraphic excavation.

In the late 19th century, the study of archaeology was professionalized and archaeological societies were established. The American Anthropological Association was founded in 1902 and the Society for American Archaeology was founded in 1935.

Archaeology has since grown to become an important field of research. It has allowed us to gain insights into cultures and civilizations of the past and to gain a better understanding of our own history. The study of archaeology has also contributed to the preservation of cultural heritage sites around the world.

DISCIPLINES OF ARCHAEOLOGY

1. ANTHROPOLOGY

Anthropology is the study of human societies and cultures, through the use of qualitative and quantitative methods. Anthropologists use a variety of methods to study the behaviour and lifeways of past and present cultures, including archaeological, ethnographic, and historical methods. Archaeology is a sub-discipline of anthropology that focuses on the study of past human cultures and societies, through the recovery, analysis and interpretation of material remains, such as artifacts, architecture, and ecofacts.

Archaeology is informed by anthropology, and the two fields have become increasingly intertwined over time. Anthropology can provide archaeologists with a better understanding of past societies and the development of human behaviour and culture over time. Anthropological research can provide archaeologists with insight into the lifeways of past peoples, allowing them to make better interpretations of the material remains they uncover. Anthropological data can also be used to supplement archaeological interpretations, and to provide support for or challenge existing archaeological theories.

In addition, archaeological data can provide anthropologists with additional information to supplement other types of anthropological research, such as linguistic analysis or ethnohistorical research.

Overall, anthropology is an invaluable tool for archaeologists, providing them with a wealth of data and evidence that can be used to gain insight into the development of human cultures and societies over time.

2. GEOGRAPHY

Geography is an important factor in archaeology, as it helps to identify where particular sites are located in relation to each other and to the environment. Geography can help archaeologists understand how past societies interacted with the landscape and can provide clues as to where they lived and travelled. For example, by studying the physical features of a landscape, such as rivers, mountains, and coastlines, archaeologists can determine how a particular culture interacted with its environment.

Geography can also help to provide clues about a particular region's climate, soil type, and other environmental factors, which can provide useful information about the past. Archaeologists can use this information to draw conclusions about the lifestyles of ancient peoples and the resources they had access to.

By studying the surrounding landscape and any existing features, such as roads, rivers, or hills, archaeologists can better determine where a site is located and how large it is. This can be especially useful in determining the size and scope of ancient settlements or cities.

3. GEO-ARCHAEOLOGY

Geo-archaeology is the study of the physical environment of archaeological sites and its relationship to the behaviour and lifeways of ancient peoples. Geo-archaeology is an important tool for understanding the environment of past societies, and can provide valuable insight into the relationships between the physical environment and the behaviour of ancient peoples.

4. STRATIGRAPHY

Stratigraphy is an important tool used in archaeology to understand the chronology of a site. It is the study of the order in which layers of sediment and artifacts were deposited in an archaeological site. Stratigraphic excavation is the process of unearthing these layers in a systematic way, while recording their position and content. Stratigraphy helps archaeologists to identify the phases of construction, occupation, and abandonment of a site. It also helps to ascertain the age of the artifacts and to determine their relative chronology.

The key to stratigraphic excavation is the recognition of layer boundaries and their relationship to one another. Each layer is assigned a number, and each artifact within the layer is also given a number to indicate its depth relative to the layer top or bottom. Stratigraphic excavation helps archaeologists to distinguish between natural and cultural deposits. Natural deposits may include geological layers, such as soil and sediment, while cultural deposits are the remains of human activity.

5. PALAEONTOLOGY

Palaeontology and archaeology are two distinct branches of the study of the past, but the two are closely related and often overlap. Palaeontology is the study of ancient life through the study of fossils, while archaeology is the study of human activity in the past through the recovery and analysis of material culture.

Palaeontology has an important role to play in archaeology. Fossils provide an insight into the past, both in terms of the evolution of organisms and the environment in which they lived. By looking at the fossils of ancient animals and plants, archaeologists can build a picture of the environment in which humans lived in the past.

Fossils can also provide clues about the development of technology in the past. By examining the fossilized remains of ancient tools and weapons, archaeologists can gain insight into the types of tools and weapons that were used by people in the past.

In addition, fossils can provide information about the dietary habits of humans in the past. By analysing the fossilized remains of animals and plants, archaeologists can gain insight into what people ate in the past and how they obtained their food. This can provide valuable insight into the diets of ancient people and the sustainability of their food sources.

6. TAPHONOMY

Taphonomy is the study of the physical and chemical changes in organisms over time. In archaeology, it is used to study the changes that have occurred in the remains of human artefacts, such as bones, teeth, and tools, over time.

Taphonomy is used to trace the history of the artefacts and provide clues about how they were used or treated. For example, if a bone from an animal is found in an archaeological site, taphonomy can be used to determine how long the animal has been dead, what kinds of conditions the environment was like when the animal died, and what type of activity the animal was involved in. This can be useful in determining the diet of the people who lived in the area.

Taphonomy can also help archaeologists to determine the cause of death for the artefacts. Studies of the bones, teeth, and tools can provide clues as to whether an animal was killed by humans or by natural causes. This can help archaeologists to determine if the people living in the area were hunters and gatherers or if they practiced agriculture.

Taphonomy can also be used to investigate the use of certain artefacts. Studies of the wear patterns on tools and weapons can provide clues as to how they were used and how frequently they were used. This can help archaeologists to determine the lifestyle of the people who used them.

7. GEOPHYSICAL METHOD

Geophysical methods are non-invasive techniques used to investigate the subsurface of the earth, which is especially useful in archaeology. Geophysical methods have been used in archaeology since the 1950s and have gained popularity in recent years due to increasing technological developments. They can provide information on the location and form of archaeological features without the need to excavate and can be used in areas where excavation would be too costly or destructive. Geophysical methods study the physical properties of the subsurface. These methods include magnetic, electrical, and ground-penetrating radar (GPR) surveys, which can be used to detect and map subsurface features.

Geophysical methods can also be used to detect, map, and study archaeological features. They can detect buried walls, foundations, and other structures, as well as artifacts such as pottery and coins. Geophysical methods can also be used to map the extent of archaeological sites and to identify areas of archaeological potential. They can be used to identify the location and extent of buried features, such as building foundations, which can be used to reconstruct the layout of an archaeological site.

Geophysical methods can also be used to study the hydrological properties of archaeological sites. Groundwater surveys measure the electrical conductivity of the subsurface, which can be used to identify areas of groundwater flow. This can be used to identify areas where archaeological features are likely to be located and to map the hydrological features of an archaeological site.

Geophysical methods provide information on the subsurface structure, archaeological features, and hydrological characteristics of an archaeological site without the need to excavate. This are increasingly being used to study archaeological sites, and they will continue to be an important tool for archaeologists in the future.

8. CHEMISTRY

Chemistry plays a major role in helping archaeologists to study and analyze the remains of the past. It can help provide us with information about the environment, diet, and diseases of ancient people. It can help determine the age of artifacts and to shed light on the history and culture of civilizations that have long been forgotten.

Chemistry can provide clues to the past in many ways. For example, carbon-14 dating is used to determine the age of artifacts. This is achieved by using the fact that all living things absorb carbon-14 from the atmosphere. When an organism dies, the amount of carbon-14 it contains begins to decrease steadily over time. By measuring the amount of carbon-14 present in an artifact, an archaeologist can estimate its age. This technique has been used to date artifacts from many different time periods, including the Stone Age, Ancient Egypt, and the Aztec Empire.

Chemistry can also be used to analyze the composition of artifacts. By studying the materials used to make them, archaeologists can gain insight into the technology and techniques used by ancient people. For example, the chemical composition of pottery can provide clues about the type of clay used, the temperatures used to fire it, and the methods used to decorate it. This information can help to better understand the culture and lifestyle of the people who created the artifacts.

Chemistry can also help archaeologists understand the environment in which ancient people lived. By studying the composition of soils and plants, archaeologists can gain insight into the climate and resources available to ancient civilizations. This information can help to explain why certain civilizations flourished while others declined.

By analyzing the chemical composition of bones and teeth, archaeologists can determine the types of foods that people ate. This can provide insight into the types of crops and animals that were available to them, as well as their overall health.

9. PHYSICS

Physics has become a vital tool for archaeologists in recent years, helping them to uncover, study and understand archaeological sites. Physics is used in all stages of the archaeological process, from exploring new sites, to analyzing artifacts and studying the remains of ancient civilizations.

Exploring new sites: Physics is used to help archaeologists explore new sites. Geophysical surveys, such as ground-penetrating radar, magnetic gradiometry, and electrical resistivity can be used to create a map of a site before excavation begins. These surveys can reveal objects and features that are buried beneath the surface, such as walls, hearths, and burials. This helps archaeologists to plan their excavations more efficiently and to identify areas of interest that may contain artifacts.

Analysis of artifacts: Physics is also used to analyze artifacts. X-ray fluorescence and X-ray diffraction can be used to identify the composition of artifacts, such as pottery and metal objects. These techniques can provide valuable information about the origin and age of artifacts. They can also reveal details about the manufacturing process, such as the temperatures used and the amount of chemicals present.

Studying the remains of ancient civilizations: Physics can also be used to study the remains of ancient civilizations. Magnetic and electrical resistivity tomography can be used to create a three-dimensional map of a site. This can reveal details about the layout of a settlement and can help to identify structures such as homes and temples. In addition, remote sensing techniques such as aerial photography and satellite imagery can be used to map large areas of land, allowing archaeologists to identify sites and features that may have been hidden from view.

10. BIOLOGY

Biology plays an increasingly important role in archaeological research, providing a range of methods for understanding the past. Archaeology is the study of human activity in the past, and biology is the study of life, so it is no surprise that the two have become intertwined.

Biological remains such as bones, teeth, and hair provide clues to the age, sex, diet, and lifestyle of a person. By studying these remains, archaeologists can gain insights into the lives of people in the past. They can also determine the cause of death and identify medical conditions, which can help to understand the health of a population.

Another way that biology helps in archaeology is through the analysis of plant and animal remains. Plant remains can provide information about the environment, such as the types of vegetation that were present in the past. Animal remains can provide information about subsistence strategies and the types of animals that were hunted or consumed.

DNA analysis is another way in which biology can be used in archaeology. By analyzing ancient DNA, archaeologists can gain insights into the genetic history of a population and how it has changed over time. This can help to understand human migration patterns and the origins of a population. It can also be used to study the genetic relationships between populations, as well as the genetic consequences of interbreeding.

Kinds Of Archaeology

A. Archaeology On The Basis Of Work

1. Environmental Archaeology

Environmental archaeology is a sub-discipline of archaeology that focuses on the study of past environments and the human activities that took place in them. Its purpose is to reconstruct past landscapes, climate, and subsistence strategies. It involves the analysis of archaeological evidence, such as animal bones and plant remains. It is an interdisciplinary field and draws on methods from various sciences such as biology, botany, palaeontology, and geology.

Environmental archaeology is important for understanding how human societies interacted with their environment and how they adapted to changing conditions over time. In addition, it can help us learn about the subsistence strategies and technologies used by past societies, as well as their impact on the environment.

Environmental archaeology can also provide information about past environmental conditions such as climate, vegetation, and animal populations. This can help us to understand how past societies adapted to their environment and how their actions affected their environment.

2. Ethno-Archaeology

Ethnoarchaeology is an archaeological research method that involves the study of living societies and cultures. It is a relatively new branch of archaeology which combines the traditional archaeological methods of excavation and analysis with the ethnographic approach of studying living cultures. Ethnoarchaeology utilizes the idea that modern societies can provide a means of understanding past societies and the archaeological record. It seeks to understand how ancient people interacted with their environment, created and used artifacts, and organized and maintained their societies.

Ethnoarchaeology is based on the premise that the material culture of a living society can be used to interpret the material culture of a past society. By studying modern societies, archaeologists can gain insights into past patterns and practices, as well as uncover information about the lifeways and cultures of past peoples.

3. SETTLEMENT ARCHAEOLOGY AND SPATIAL ANALYSIS

Settlement archaeology and spatial analysis are interrelated sub-disciplines of archaeology that focus on the study of human settlements. Settlement archaeology focuses on the analysis of the physical remains of past settlements, while spatial analysis is an analytical approach used to examine the spatial relationships between different elements within a settlement.

Settlement archaeology is concerned with the physical remains of past settlements, such as dwellings, fortifications, and other structures. It also includes evidence of the activities and lifestyle of the inhabitants, such as artifacts, tools, and other material remains. Settlement archaeology seeks to reconstruct past human settlements and to understand how they were organized and used.

Spatial analysis is an analytical approach used to examine the spatial relationships between different elements within a settlement. It involves mapping the physical remains of past settlements and analyzing the patterns created by the various elements. It also involves studying the relationships between the different elements in order to gain an understanding of how the settlement was organized and used.

It can also provide insights into the social and economic relationships between different elements of a settlement. This can be used to gain a better understanding of past human societies and the ways in which they interacted and adapted to their environment.

4. LANDSCAPE ARCHAEOLOGY

Landscape archaeology is a subfield of archaeology that studies the physical and cultural landscape of a given area. It is an interdisciplinary approach that merges archaeological evidence with historical documents, geography, geology, and ecology. Landscape archaeology seeks to understand how people interacted with their environment and how it changed over time.

It examines the relationship between people and their physical environment, including the ways in which they used the land and how it shaped their culture and identity. Landscape archaeology also examines how people represented and experienced their environment, and how this environment changed over time. It allows us to gain an understanding of how different cultures have interacted with their environment in the past, and can help us to better understand our own relationships with the land today.

5. HOUSEHOLD ARCHAEOLOGY

Household archaeology is the study of the everyday lives of ancient people through the remains of their dwellings. It is the study of the material culture of households, such as the tools and objects used in everyday life. Household archaeology offers insights into how ancient people lived and interacted with their environment, as well as providing a glimpse into their beliefs and values.

Household archaeology typically focuses on the archaeological remains of dwellings, such as the structure of the building, the layout of the interior, and any artifacts found within the building. Household archaeology can also provide information on the division of labour within households, as well as the technology used for food production and other activities.

Household archaeology is a relatively new field of study, and its methods are still being developed. It is usually studied in conjunction with other archaeological methods, such as landscape archaeology, which examines the relationship between people and their environment.

5. CONTEXTUAL ARCHAEOLOGY

Contextual archaeology is an archaeological approach which focuses on the context in which artifacts and archaeological features are found. It seeks to understand the relationships between artifacts and the environment, as well as the inter-relationships between different artifacts and features

Contextual archaeologists focus on the study of the physical contexts of the archaeological remains, such as the landscape, soil, and sediment layers. They also look at the various artifacts and features in relation to each other, and how they fit within the overall context of the site.

6. MARXIST ARCHAEOLOGY

Marxist archaeology is an archaeological approach that seeks to understand the past through a materialist and dialectical perspective. It is informed by the writings of Karl Marx, who argued that societies are shaped by the relationship between their means of production and the underlying power dynamics of class and inequality.

Marxist archaeologists strive to uncover the ways in which people in the past used their resources and interacted with one another to create and maintain social structures. Marxist archaeology has been used to examine a range of topics including the development of early cities, the origins of inequality, and the emergence of complex societies.

It has also been used to explore how people in the past experienced oppression, exploitation, and resistance. Marxist archaeology is an important tool for understanding the past and highlighting the important role that class and inequality have played in shaping human history.

7. GENDER ARCHAEOLOGY

Gender archaeology is an approach to archaeology that focuses on understanding the roles and experiences of people of different genders within a specific culture or period. It is an interdisciplinary field that includes the study of artifacts, skeletal remains, and other archaeological evidence to understand the lives of women, men, and genderqueer people in the past.

Gender archaeology looks at the roles of gender in the formation of social, political, and economic power, and how this power was expressed through material culture. It examines the way gender and sex are represented in the archaeological record, and how it may have changed over time.

Additionally, gender archaeology is concerned with understanding how gender intersects with other forms of social identities, such as race, age, and class. It seeks to identify the ways power is distributed across different genders, and how this power has been used to shape society.

8. COGNITIVE ARCHAEOLOGY

Cognitive archaeology is an approach to archaeology that focuses on reconstructing the mental processes, beliefs, and behaviours of past societies. It is based on the idea that understanding the cognitive processes used by ancient peoples can help us to better understand their material culture and social organization.

Cognitive archaeology looks at how ancient societies used language, symbols, and other forms of communication to organize their societies and create meaning. It also examines how they used material culture, such as art and architecture, to express their beliefs and values. This approach allows archaeologists to better understand the development of cultural systems, as well as the motivations and reasons for the construction of monuments and other material culture.

9. Underwater Archaeology

Underwater archaeology is a field of study that focuses on the investigation and analysis of submerged cultural heritage sites. It is a complex and challenging field of research, which requires a combination of skills and techniques from both archaeology and diving.

Underwater archaeology looks at the remains of human activity that are found underwater, such as shipwrecks, sunken buildings, and other archaeological remains that are located at the bottom of lakes, oceans, and rivers. It is a unique form of archaeology as the archaeological remains are affected by the ever-changing environment underwater and can be heavily eroded by the water, marine life, and other natural processes.

Underwater archaeologists must use specialized equipment and methods to locate, investigate, and interpret these fragile remains. This includes the use of sonar, submersible vehicles, diving, and archaeological excavation techniques. Underwater archaeologists can use remote sensing technology to survey large areas and detect archaeological sites, as well as the use of divers to investigate sites in more detail. Underwater archaeology allows us to better understand our maritime history and gain a deeper insight into the past.

10. AVIATION ARCHAEOLOGY

Aviation archaeology is the study of aircraft and aviation-related artifacts from the past. It involves the recovery, conservation, and interpretation of aircraft and their associated remains, such as aircraft engines, armament, and other debris.

Aviation archaeologists focus on the historical context of aviation, including its impact on society, technology, and the environment. Aviation archaeologists are typically members of a local aviation history society and often engage in "fieldwork," which involves locating and recovering aircraft and their associated remains from the sites of airplane crashes. They also conduct research using archived documents, photographs, diaries, and other records. In addition, they work with local communities to help preserve and interpret aviation artifacts, such as memorials and monuments, aviation art, and other artifacts.

Aviation archaeology also involves the use of Geographic Information Systems (GIS) to map and analyze aviation-related data, such as aircraft crash sites. This helps archaeologists better understand the context and significance of aviation-related events and artifacts.

Additionally, aviation archaeologists collaborate with scientists and engineers to study aircraft design and technology. This includes analyzing and reconstructing aircraft designs, examining the performance of aircraft components, and studying the causes of aircraft accidents.

11. Aerial Archaeology

Aerial archaeology is the use of aerial photography and other remote sensing techniques to identify and map archaeological sites or features from the air. Aerial survey allows archaeologists to map features in the landscape that may not be visible from the ground, such as cropmarks and soil marks.

Aerial archaeology is often used in combination with ground survey and excavation. The aerial images are used to identify potential sites which are then inspected more closely on the ground. The images can also be used to detect changes in the landscape over time, and to identify areas of disturbance which may indicate human activity.

Aerial archaeology is particularly useful in areas where the landscape has been disturbed by modern activities such as urban development, farming and forestry. It can be used to identify and map archaeological features which may otherwise be obscured or destroyed.

Aerial archaeology can also be used to detect changes in the landscape over long periods of time. By comparing aerial photographs taken at different times, archaeologists can map the evolution of a site over time and identify areas of long-term human activity.

12. Industrial Archaeology

Industrial archaeology is the study of the physical remains of industrial activity, from the past to the present. It focuses on the sites, structures, artifacts, and other tangible evidence of technological, economic, and social change caused by industrialization. Industrial archaeology examines how and why industries evolved, how they changed the landscape, and the impact they had on society. It also looks at the impact of industrialization on the environment, and how that has been addressed over time.

Industrial archaeology can include the study of mills, factories, mines, railways, canals, and other industrial sites. It also includes the study of industrial artifacts, such as machinery, tools, and documents. Industrial archaeology provides an understanding of how people and industry have interacted over time, and helps to explain how industrialization has changed our lives.

13. EXPERIMENTAL ARCHAEOLOGY

Experimental archaeology is a field of archaeology that uses modern techniques to investigate the past. It involves the replication of ancient technologies, tools, and structures to test hypotheses on how they were used and created. It also helps to provide a more accurate interpretation of archaeological evidence by providing hands-on experience of ancient technologies. This type of archaeology is useful in reconstructing lifeways and technologies of ancient societies.

Examples of experimental archaeology include building replica structures, making pottery and tools, and even trying out ancient methods of hunting and fishing. Through experimental archaeology, archaeologists can gain a better understanding of ancient societies and the processes that shaped them.

14. SALVAGE OR RESCUE ARCHAEOLOGY

Salvage archaeology, also known as rescue archaeology, is a process by which archaeological sites are investigated and recorded prior to being destroyed by natural processes, human activities, and/or development projects. It is often used as a method of prevention and protection of archaeological sites from destruction, and to preserve and document the sites before they are destroyed or altered.

Salvage archaeology is usually conducted in response to some kind of development or construction project. The archaeological sites are usually investigated, documented, and recorded prior to the start of the project. This allows for the preservation of the sites and the artifacts that are found. The data collected is then used to inform further research and to provide a better understanding of the past.

The process of salvage archaeology involves survey and excavation of the sites, and the recovery of artifacts and features. The artifacts and features are then analysed and used to provide information about the past. The data is then used to develop a better understanding of the history, culture, and technology of the region.

15. BATTLEFIELD ARCHAEOLOGY

Battlefield archaeology is a branch of archaeology that focuses on the remains of military sites and battles. It is primarily concerned with identifying, dating, and interpreting the physical remains of warfare and conflict. Battlefield archaeologists use a range of methods to collect data, including surveys, excavations, and the analysis of historic documents. Archaeologists who specialize in this field can often help to explain the events that took place during a battle, as well as to reveal the layout and tactics that were used by the opposing forces.

Battlefield archaeology can tell us a great deal about the history of conflicts and the strategies that were employed by both sides. Battlefield archaeology also helps to preserve the memory of those who lost their lives in battle, as well as to honour their courage and sacrifice.

16. Commercial Archaeology

Commercial archaeology is the practice of archaeology for profit or commercial gain. It is the branch of archaeology that applies archaeological methods and techniques to answer questions or solve problems of a commercial or business nature. It is used to evaluate and mitigate archaeological sites that may be affected by development projects. This type of archaeology often works in conjunction with engineering, construction, and other fields.

Commercial archaeology is focused on the management, mitigation, and preservation of archaeological sites. It uses a variety of methods, such as field surveys, testing, data collection, remote sensing, and laboratory analysis.

Commercial archaeology also includes research and analysis of historic and cultural resources. Archaeologists use a variety of methods to document and interpret sites and artifacts. This interpretation can be used to inform and enhance public understanding and appreciation of the past.

17. Forensic Archaeology

Forensic archaeology is the application of archaeological methods and techniques to the investigation of criminal cases. It is a specialized field within the discipline of archaeology that requires a unique set of skills and knowledge. It also requires an understanding of the legal system and the ability to identify, collect, process and analyze evidence in a manner that will be accepted in a court of law.

Forensic archaeologists use a variety of methods and techniques to search for evidence. These include ground penetrating radar, metal detectors, magnetic mapping and aerial photography. They also use soil science and stratigraphic analysis to determine the sequence of events at a crime scene.

Forensic archaeologists are also responsible for documenting their findings. This includes taking photographs and notes, creating maps and sketches of the scene and collecting any evidence found. They also need to be able to accurately interpret the evidence that they have collected and present it in a way that is both understandable and persuasive to a court of law.

B. Archaeology On The Basis Of Historic Time Period

1. Prehistoric Archaeology

Prehistoric archaeology is the study of the ancient past, using material remains from before the invention of writing. This includes artifacts, architecture, landscapes, and environmental remains. This type of archaeology relies heavily on the use of technology and scientific methods to recover and analyze data from the past.

Prehistoric archaeologists often use excavation techniques to uncover remains, as well as laboratory analysis, remote sensing, and other techniques to examine and interpret the recovered material. They also often collaborate with other disciplines, such as palaeontology, anthropology, and geology, to gain a better understanding of the past. Prehistoric archaeology is important in helping to reconstruct past societies and understand the history of humanity. It can also provide insight into the development of early technologies, the interaction of different cultures, and the impact of environmental change on ancient peoples.

2. Protohistoric Archaeology

Protohistoric archaeology is the study of the period of time in which humans moved away from the hunter-gatherer lifestyle and began using more complex forms of subsistence strategies, such as the domestication of animals and plants. This period of time is known as the transition from prehistory to history. It falls between the end of the Neolithic period and the beginning of written records.

Protohistoric archaeology focuses on the material culture of this time period. This includes the investigation of monuments, settlements, and artifacts that are used to examine a variety of aspects of the past, including social organization, subsistence strategies, and technological developments. It also involves studying the material evidence from the transition from prehistory to history, which can provide insights into the process of state formation.

Protohistoric archaeology has been used to study a variety of societies, from ancient Rome to the Mississippian period in North America. It is a valuable tool for reconstructing past societies, understanding changes in human behaviour during the transition to state formation, and for helping to explain the development of complex societies.

3. HISTORICAL ARCHAEOLOGY

Historical archaeology is the study of the material remains of past human societies that have been left behind in the archaeological record. It integrates the traditional archaeological techniques of excavation, analysis and interpretation with the written record to uncover the history of past societies.

Historical archaeology covers a great deal of time, from the earliest evidence of humans to the present day. It can be used to explore a wide range of topics, including the material culture of a particular period, the environment and the lives of people living in the past.

Historical archaeology is an interdisciplinary field, incorporating elements of material culture, anthropology, history, geology and other disciplines. It can provide a unique insight into the past, as it often reveals details that are not present in the written record, such as the presence of former inhabitants and their daily practices.

4. CLASSICAL ARCHAEOLOGY

Classical archaeology is a branch of archaeology that focuses on the material culture and physical remains of the classical world from the 8th century BCE to the 6th century CE. It studies the physical remains of the ancient Greek, Roman, and Near Eastern civilizations, including monuments, pottery, sculpture, coins, and other artifacts.

Classical archaeologists use these artifacts to reconstruct the social and political history of the ancient world. They also use them to understand how these ancient cultures interacted and how they influenced each other. Classical archaeology has been used to shed light on the rise and fall of empires, the spread of religious belief systems, and the development of technology.

5. MEDIEVAL AND MODERN ARCHAEOLOGY

Medieval archaeology focuses on the material culture of the period between the 5th and 15th centuries CE. It looks at the ruins of castles, monasteries, and other structures, as well as art and artifacts associated with medieval life. It also examines the social and economic structures of the period.

Modern archaeology is the archaeological study of the period from the 16th century to the present. It looks at more recent ruins, such as factories and buildings from the industrial revolution, as well as art and artifacts from the modern world. It considers the social and economic structures of the period and how they have changed over time. Modern archaeology also incorporates scientific techniques such as radiocarbon dating and DNA analysis.

PROCESS OF ARCHAEOLOGY

Process of Archaeology includes in various steps as follows:

STEP 1: RESEARCH AND PLANNING

Archaeological research involves the collection and analysis of material culture to gain a better understanding of past societies and cultures. Planning in archaeology involves creating strategies for conducting research, including determining which methods are to be used, what data to collect, and how to analyze the data.

STEP 2: SURVEY AND MAPPING

Survey and mapping in archaeology involves the systematic observation and recording of archaeological sites and features. This includes photographing, measuring, and mapping archaeological features in order to create an accurate and detailed record of the site.

STEP 3: EXCAVATION

Excavation in archaeology is the process of recovering artifacts and other archaeological remains from the ground. This is done through careful removal of soil and other layers in order to uncover and document the remains of past societies and cultures.

STEP 4: ANALYSIS

Analysis in archaeology is the process of studying artifacts, ecofacts, and other archaeological remains in order to interpret their significance and meaning. This involves using a range of methods and techniques, including typological analysis, stratigraphic analysis, and spatial analysis.

STEP 5: INTERPRETATION

Interpretation in archaeology is the process of making sense of archaeological data in order to gain a better understanding of past societies and cultures. This involves analyzing artifacts, ecofacts, and other remains, as well as considering the context in which they were found.

STEP 6: CONSERVATION AND PRESERVATION

Conservation and preservation in archaeology involves the protection of archaeological sites and artifacts through the use of preventive measures, such as the development of management plans, and the use of conservation and restoration techniques.

STEP 7: PUBLIC OUTREACH

Public outreach in archaeology involves engaging and educating the public on archaeological topics, such as the importance of heritage conservation, the ethical conduct of research, and the significance of archaeological finds. This often includes the use of media and public lectures, as well as museum exhibitions and educational programs.

Let's discuss the above processes in detail in the upcoming lessons.

Research And Planning

Archaeological research and planning can be divided into two main types:

1. **Survey-based** research involves studying the surface of a site in order to identify artifacts and other evidence of past human activity. This type of research is used to gain a broad understanding of a site and its history.
2. **Excavation-based** research involves digging into the ground in order to uncover artifacts, buildings, and other features that may have been buried or otherwise hidden away. This type of research is used to gain an in-depth understanding of a site and its history.

Archaeological research and planning involves several other methods and techniques. These can include field surveys, aerial photography, geophysical surveys, laboratory analysis, and more.

Field surveys involve walking across the land, looking for artifacts and other evidence of past human activity. Aerial photography and geophysical surveys use imaging techniques to detect features that may not be visible at ground level. Laboratory analysis includes examining artifacts, soils, and other materials to determine their age, composition, and other characteristics.

In addition to these methods, archaeologists may also use historical sources, archival research, and other resources to gain a better understanding of the past. They may also use computer-aided design and Geographic Information Systems (GIS) to map and visualize data.

The data gathered through these methods and techniques is then used to develop research questions, hypotheses, and research plans. These can help archaeologists to understand the past in more detail and develop more effective ways of preserving and interpreting the past.

The **first step** in the process is to develop a research question. This question is often based on a specific hypothesis or a set of hypotheses that the archaeologist wants to test. The research question determines the scope of the project and the types of data that need to be collected.

The **second step** is to develop a research plan. This plan outlines the methods and techniques that will be used to collect the data, as well as the timeline and budget for the project. The plan should also include a description of the types of data to be collected and how they will be analysed.

The **third step** is to gather the necessary data. This includes field work, laboratory analysis, and other research activities. The data collected should be used to answer the research question.

The **fourth step** is to analyze the data. This involves organizing and interpreting the data in order to draw meaningful conclusions. This step is often done using statistical methods, such as regression analysis.

Finally, the results of the project should be reported in a written form. This report should include a description of the research question, the methods and techniques used, the results, and any conclusions or recommendations.

SURVEY AND MAPPING

Survey and mapping in archaeology is a process used to collect data about an archaeological site, which can then be used to create a map of the site. This process involves collecting information about the location, orientation, and shape of archaeological features and artifacts, as well as measuring and recording the depth, orientation, and size of any features or artifacts found. This data can then be used to create a map of the site, which can be used to better understand the archaeological context of the site and the artifacts found there.

Survey and mapping in archaeology is an essential part of any archaeological research project. Maps of archaeological sites can help archaeologists to better understand the archaeological context of the site and plan their excavations. Surveys and maps can also help to protect and preserve archaeological sites by providing detailed information about the site.

Survey and mapping in archaeology is typically done using a range of tools and techniques, *including aerial photography, remote sensing, and Geographic Information System (GIS) technology.*

Aerial photography, for example, can be used to capture images of the site from above, providing archaeologists with an overview of the site and any features or artifacts present.

Remote sensing, such as lidar, can be used to scan and map the surface of the site and create a detailed 3D model. GIS technology can be used to layer data, such as terrain information and aerial photos, and create detailed maps of the site.

Survey and mapping in archaeology can also be done using ground surveys, which involve recording the location, orientation, and size of any features or artifacts found on the surface of the site.

Ground surveys can also be used to take measurements and record the depth of any artifacts found. Ground surveys are typically done using a range of tools, such as tape measures, compasses, trowels, and shovels.

METHODS IN SURVEY AND MAPPING

1. GEO-PHYSIC TECHNIQUE

Geo-physic techniques are a suite of non-invasive surveys used to collect data about the subsurface of an archaeological site. These techniques are used to detect the presence of buried archaeological features, such as foundations, walls, and artifacts. The data collected can be used to inform research questions, to aid in the interpretation of archaeological remains, or to plan for the excavation of a site.

I.   The first step in the process of geo-physic technique is to select the type of survey that is best suited for the archaeological site.

The most common types of survey are magnetometry, ground penetrating radar (GPR), and electrical resistivity tomography (ERT). Each of these techniques provides data about the subsurface in a different way, so it is important to select the technique that will provide the best data for the research questions.

II.   Once the type of survey is selected, the survey team will need to plan the survey. This includes determining the survey area, the scale of the survey, and the desired resolution of the data.

It is also important to decide how the data will be collected—by hand or with a machine—and the type of equipment that will be used. The survey team will also need to identify any potential hazards, such as power lines or underground infrastructure, that could interfere with the survey.

III.	Once the survey has been planned, the survey team can begin collecting data. With magnetometry, the survey team will use a magnetometer to measure the magnetic field of the subsurface.

With **GPR** (Ground Penetrating Radar), the team will send radar pulses into the subsurface and measure the reflected signals.

With **ERT** (Electrical Resistance Tomography), the team will measure the electrical resistance of the subsurface.

IV.	Once the data has been collected, the survey team will process the data and create a map of the subsurface. This map can be used to identify areas of interest, such as buried features or artifacts.

V.	The survey team can then use this map to plan the excavation of the site or to inform other research questions.

Techniques of Detection in Archaeological Geophysics	
Method	**Frequency of Use**
Electrical Resistance	High
Magnetometry	High
Electromagnetic	Mid/Low
Magnetic Susceptibility	Mid/Low
Metal Detectors	Mid/Low
Ground Penetrating Radar	High/Mid
Seismic	Low
Microgravity	Low
Induced Polarisation	Low
Self-Potential	Low
Thermal	Low

2. GEOGRAPHIC INFORMATION SYSTEM (GIS)

Geographic Information Systems (GIS) has emerged as a powerful tool for archaeological research. GIS combines the principles of cartography, spatial analysis, and information technology to create an interactive and visual platform to analyze and display spatial data.

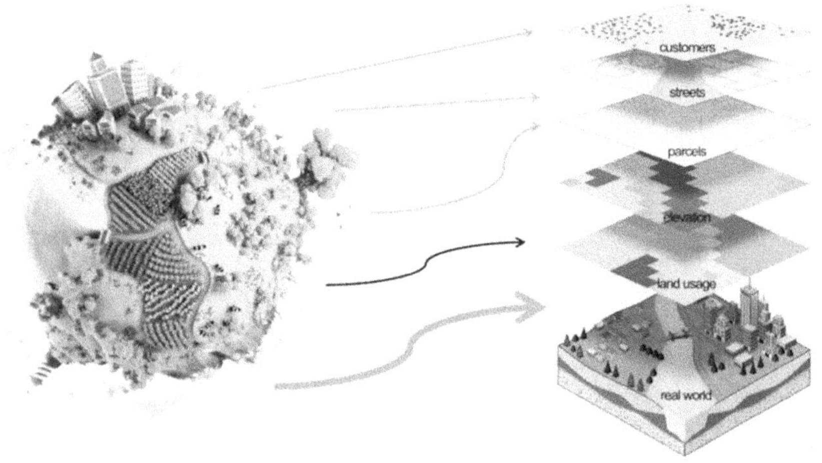

GIS can be used to create detailed maps of archaeological sites, analyze spatial relationships between sites and features, and model past environments and landscapes.

I.   The basic process of GIS in archaeology begins with data collection. Archaeologists collect various types of data from the field, such as artifacts, soil samples, and photographs.

II.   All of this data is digitized and inputted into the GIS system. This data can then be used to create maps, which are then used to analyze spatial relationships between sites and features.

III.   The next step of GIS involves creating a map. Maps are created by inputting points, lines, and polygons into the GIS system.

Points represent individual features, such as archaeological sites or artifacts.

Lines represent linear features, such as pathways or roads.

Polygons represent areas, such as boundaries or features in a landscape.

Maps are also created using satellite imagery and aerial photography, which can provide a detailed view of an area.

IV.   Once the map is created, it can be used to analyze spatial relationships. GIS can be used to calculate distances between points, calculate the area of polygons, and identify patterns and clusters of features. This can be used to identify relationships between sites and features, such as the proximity of sites to water sources or the relationship between sites and topography.

GIS can also be used to model past environments and landscapes. By inputting data on past climates, vegetation, and soils, GIS can be used to create models of past environments and landscapes. This can be used to identify potential locations for archaeological sites, study the impact of climate change on sites, and reconstruct ancient landscapes.

V.   Finally, GIS can be used to create detailed visualizations and simulations. By combining GIS data with 3D visualization software, archaeologists can create detailed 3D simulations of archaeological sites and landscapes. This can be used to study the architecture of sites, visualize past environments, or create immersive virtual tours of sites.

3. TOTAL STATION MAPPING

Total station mapping is a tool used in archaeological fieldwork to record the spatial position of archaeological features, artefacts and other finds. It is used to map the layout of archaeological sites, as well as to accurately record the position and dimensions of archaeological features.

Total station mapping is a powerful tool that helps archaeologists to accurately record and interpret the data they collect in the field. Total station mapping involves the use of a total station, which is an instrument that combines an electronic distance measuring device (EDM) with an angular measuring device (theodolite).

I.   The EDM uses an infrared laser to measure the distance between the total station and a point on the ground, while the theodolite measures the horizontal and vertical angle of the total station relative to the point on the ground.

II.   In total station mapping, the total station is set up in a fixed position and then pointed towards a point on the ground.

III.   The point is then identified using a prism or a reflector, which reflects the laser beam back to the total station.

The total station records the distance to the point and the angle of the total station relative to the point.

IV.   This data is then used to calculate the exact position of the point (x, y, z coordinates) in three-dimensional space.

V.   Once the position of the point has been recorded, the total station can then be moved to a new position and the process repeated.

VI.   By repeating this process at a number of points, an accurate map of the archaeological site can be created.

4. REMOTE SENSING

Remote sensing is the use of technology to collect and analyze data from the environment at a distance. This technology has been widely used in archaeology to study and document archaeological sites.

Remote sensing techniques utilize satellite and aerial imagery to identify, map and study archaeological sites. By using various sensors, archaeologists can "see" features that may not be visible to the naked eye, such as buried structures, roads, and artifacts. The data collected can then be used to create maps and reconstruct the past.

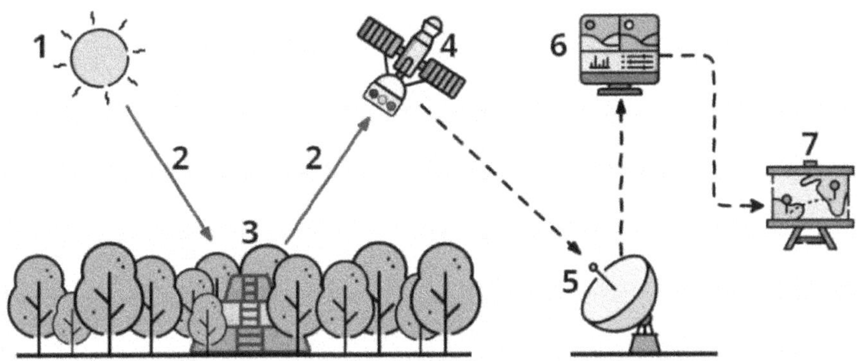

One of the most common remote sensing techniques used in archaeology is **aerial photography**. This technique involves photographing the landscape from an airplane or helicopter. By using a camera to take pictures from different angles, archaeologists can identify features that may be hidden from the ground. Aerial photography is especially useful for studying large archaeological sites, as it can capture a wide area in a single image.

Another common remote sensing technique used in archaeology is **LiDAR (Light Detection and Ranging).** This technology uses a laser to measure the distance between an object and the sensor. By measuring the time it takes for the laser to travel to the object and back, LiDAR can create a 3D model of the site. This model can be used to identify and map buried structures, as well as to measure their size and shape.

Finally, **satellite imagery** is another remote sensing technique used in archaeology. Satellite imagery uses sensors to take pictures of the Earth from space. Satellite imagery can also be used to create maps of large archaeological sites, which can be used to plan excavations.

Excavation

In archaeology, excavation is the process of removing archaeological materials (such as artifacts, ecofacts, and features) from the ground for analysis and interpretation. Excavation involves removing layers of soil and sediment, sometimes with the aid of mechanical tools, in order to reveal remains from the past. Archaeologists carefully extract, map, and record the location of artifacts, ecofacts, and features, taking into account the landscapes in which they are found.

The goal of excavation is to uncover evidence of the past in order to understand how humans, animals, or plants interacted with the environment. Excavation is one of the most important tools used by archaeologists to gather data and form interpretations about past cultures and societies. It is an essential part of the archaeological process and allows researchers to reconstruct past lifeways and environments.

Excavations can be conducted in a variety of ways depending on the context, purpose, and goals of the excavation. Archaeologists typically begin by surveying the site, mapping its features, and taking pictures of the area. Once the area has been surveyed, archaeologists can determine the best way to excavate the site. This could include hand excavation, the use of mechanical tools, or a combination of the two. During excavation, archaeologists use data recording techniques to accurately document the way in which each artifact, feature, or ecofacts was discovered.

The excavation of archaeological sites requires careful planning and management to ensure that valuable information is not lost or destroyed.

METHODS USED FOR EXCAVATION

1. STRIP EXCAVATION

Strip excavation is a method used in archaeology that involves removing a layer of soil in strips or layers to explore a site. It is often used when archaeologists want to make a detailed study of a site and to better understand the sequence of activities that may have occurred there.

I. Strip excavation begins by staking out the boundaries of the site. This can be done by using a string line, which is a string that is held between two points.

II. The stakes are then used to mark the boundaries of the site.

III. Once the boundaries are marked, the archaeologist will begin the excavation process by removing a strip of soil. In some cases, a trench may be dug at the beginning to expose the first layer.

The depth of the strip excavation can vary based on the size of the site and what the archaeologist is looking for.

IV. The soil from the strip is then examined for archaeological evidence. This includes artifacts, such as pottery, tools, and bones, as well as features like postholes and fire pits. Any artifacts or features that are found are documented and mapped.

V.   The soil itself is also analysed for features such as colour and texture, which can help to identify changes in the environment of the site.

VI.   The strip excavation is then repeated, with the archaeologist moving down the site in strips. As the site is excavated, a plan of the site can be drawn up showing the location of all of the artifacts and features. This plan helps the archaeologist to understand how the site may have changed over time.

Strip excavation is an important tool for archaeologists, as it provides a detailed look at a site. It helps archaeologists to better understand the sequence of activities that may have occurred at the site.

2. BLOCK EXCAVATION

Block excavation is an archaeological technique used to uncover and study remains of archaeological sites. This method is used to isolate and record specific areas of the site  being studied, and it can be used to reveal information about a site's chronology, the composition of the site, and the use of the site.

I.   The first step in block excavation is to determine the size of the excavation area. This can be done by taking into account the size of the archaeological site itself and the size of the excavation unit.

The excavation unit is the area that will be excavated and it is typically much smaller than the entire site. The excavation unit should be determined based on the size and complexity of the site and the goals of the excavation.

II.   Once the excavation unit has been determined, the archaeologists must then divide the unit into smaller blocks.

The blocks should be uniform in size and shape, so that the excavation can proceed in a systematic manner. The blocks should also be located in such a way that the archaeologists can access them easily and record the information gathered from each block.

III.   The archaeologists then begin to excavate each block using a variety of techniques. These techniques include hand excavation, mechanical excavation, and the use of specialized archaeological tools.

During the excavation process, the archaeologists record all of the findings within each block. This includes artifacts, features, and any other evidence that is found. It is important to note any stratigraphy (the layers of a site) that may be present as this can provide valuable information about the site's chronology.

IV.   Once the excavation has been completed, the archaeologists must then analyze the findings. This includes mapping the artifacts, features, and stratigraphy, as well as examining the stratigraphy and artifacts to learn more about the site's chronology, composition, and use.

The archaeologists will also use the information gathered to create an interpretative report that can help to inform future archaeological research.

Block excavation is a valuable archaeological technique that can help to uncover and study archaeological sites. It can provide archaeologists with valuable insight into the site's chronology, composition, and use. Block excavation is used in a variety of archaeological contexts and can be used to uncover information about sites from various time periods.

3. TEST EXCAVATION

Test excavation is a procedure used in archaeology to uncover and analyze archaeological remains. It is used to determine the size, scope, and nature of a site, as well as to determine the potential of a site for further excavation. Test excavation is a key tool in the archaeological process, allowing archaeologists to make informed decisions about where to dig and how to excavate sites.

Test excavation involves a number of different steps.

I. First, archaeologists will conduct surface surveys of the site, examining the surface features and looking for artifacts that may indicate the presence of an archaeological site.

This can include looking for artifacts such as pottery shards, stone tools, or evidence of human activity such as postholes or hearths.

II. Once an area is identified as potentially containing archaeological remains, a test excavation is conducted.
III. During the test excavation, archaeologists will use various techniques to uncover and analyze the archaeological remains.

This can include techniques such as shovel testing, which involves digging small shovel pits at regular intervals across the site to uncover artifacts and features.

Archaeologists may also use larger excavation techniques, such as mechanical excavation, to uncover larger areas of the site. As the archaeologists excavate, they will record the soil layers, features, and artifacts found in order to map the site and analyze the data.

IV.   Once the test excavation is complete, archaeologists will assess the data collected. This includes analyzing the artifacts and features uncovered, as well as examining the soil layers. This analysis will help archaeologists determine the age and significance of the site and decide whether or not to proceed with further excavation.

Test excavation is an important tool in the archaeological process, allowing archaeologists to make informed decisions about where to dig and how to excavate sites. By uncovering and analyzing archaeological remains, archaeologists can gain a better understanding of the past and the people who lived in it.

4. Geo-Archaeological Excavation

Geoarchaeological excavation is an archaeological technique that uses the principles of geology and earth science to better understand the structure and context of archaeological sites. The purpose of geoarchaeological excavation is to provide a more comprehensive view of the archaeological record and to improve the accuracy of interpretations and reconstructions of human activities.

I.   Geoarchaeological excavation is a systematic process that involves the collection of samples from the archaeological site.

Samples are usually collected from the surface and from deeper layers, with the samples from deeper layers providing more detailed information about the site's stratigraphy, hydrology, climate, and geomorphic history.

II. During the collection process, archaeologists may also document a variety of features, such as the location of artifacts, the degree of soil compaction, and the presence of any geological anomalies.

III. Once the samples are collected, they are taken to a laboratory for analysis.

The analysis typically involves a variety of tests, such as measuring the physical and chemical properties of the soil, identifying pollen or other organic remains, and evaluating the presence of trace elements, such as iron or titanium.

IV. The results of the laboratory analysis are then used to reconstruct the history of the site and to provide insight into the environmental conditions in which humans interacted with their environment.

Geoarchaeological excavation can also provide information about the sources of material culture and the subsistence strategies used by past populations. For example, archaeologists may be able to identify the types of stone used to make tools and weapons, or the species of mammals and fish that were hunted for food.

In addition, geoarchaeological excavation can provide insight into how past populations interacted with their environment, such as the types of plants that were cultivated, the methods of water management, and the use of fire. The results of geoarchaeological excavation can be used to develop more accurate models of past environments and to better understand the behaviour of past populations.

5. TRENCH EXCAVATION

Trench excavation is a method of archaeological excavation used to explore the stratigraphy of a site. This method is often used to access the underlying layers of soil, which can provide important information about the site's history. Trench excavation is a labour-intensive process that requires careful planning and execution.

I. The first step in any trench excavation is to carefully plan the area to be excavated. This includes mapping out the area to be excavated, determining the size and shape of the trench, and deciding which tools and equipment will be needed.

The planning phase is also the time to consider any potential safety hazards, such as old foundations or large boulders that could be encountered during the excavation.

II. Once the area has been planned, the actual excavation can begin. The excavation team will typically start by using a shovel to dig a shallow trench. This trench is then widened and deepened with the use of a pickaxe or mattock. As the trench is deepened, the soil is carefully sifted and examined for artifacts and other evidence of past activity.

III. Once the trench has been dug to the desired depth, the team can begin to record any features that are encountered. This includes features such as postholes, wall lines, or fireplaces.

The team will typically use a tape measure and a level to record the exact dimensions and orientation of these features.

IV. Once all of the features have been recorded, the team can begin to backfill the trench. This is done carefully, with the soil being replaced in the same order that it was removed. This helps to keep the stratigraphy of the site intact, and makes post-excavation analysis easier.

Trench excavation is an important method of archaeological excavation. It allows archaeologists to access the underlying layers of soil and record the features they find.

6. HAND EXCAVATION OR TROWELLING

Hand excavation or trowelling is a method of archaeological excavation used by archaeologists to uncover and remove artifacts from a stratified archaeological site. This method is used when the soil has been disturbed, either by natural forces or by human activity. In order to uncover the artifacts, the soil must be cleared away to expose the artifact layers.

I.   The process of hand excavation begins with the selection of the site to be excavated.

The size, depth and type of artifacts to be recovered must be taken into consideration when choosing the site.

II.   Once the site has been selected, the area must be cleared of debris and vegetation. The area should also be marked out in order to identify the exact area to be excavated.

III.   In order to excavate the site, a trowel is used to remove the soil and artifacts. The trowel is used to scrape away the dirt and soil in order to uncover the artifacts. The trowel can also be used to break up and remove any rocks or other solid objects that may be in the way. As the artifacts are uncovered, they are carefully documented and labelled for further study.

IV.   Once the artifacts have been uncovered, they must be carefully examined and catalogued. This involves taking detailed notes on the artifact's size, shape, colour, texture, and condition. Photographs of the artifacts should also be taken for further study.

V.   In order to ensure that all of the artifacts are recovered, the soil must be screened.

Screening involves sifting the soil through a fine mesh screen in order to capture any small artifacts that may have been overlooked during the excavation process.

VI.   Once all of the artifacts have been recovered and documented, they must be removed from the site. The artifacts should be carefully packed in boxes or containers and labelled with the site name, location, and the date of the excavation.

Hand excavation or trowelling is a time consuming and labour-intensive process, but it is an important part of archaeological excavation. It allows archaeologists to uncover artifacts that are not visible to the naked eye, and it is essential for the recovery and preservation of artifacts from archaeological sites.

7. MECHANICAL EXCAVATION

Mechanical excavation is a technique used in archaeology to uncover buried artifacts, features, and remains of past civilizations. This method of excavation is used by archaeologists to gain a greater understanding of past societies and to gain access to deeper layers of the archaeological record than manual excavation can offer.

Mechanical excavation is often necessary when dealing with sites that have been heavily disturbed due to modern construction or human activity. Mechanical excavation can also provide access to deeper archaeological deposits and can help speed up the excavation process.

Mechanical excavation is a process that utilizes various machines and tools to excavate archaeological sites. Commonly used machines and tools include backhoes, bulldozers, bucket loaders, trenchers, and augers. Depending on the type of excavation, these machines may be used to remove soil or to move large amounts of earth.

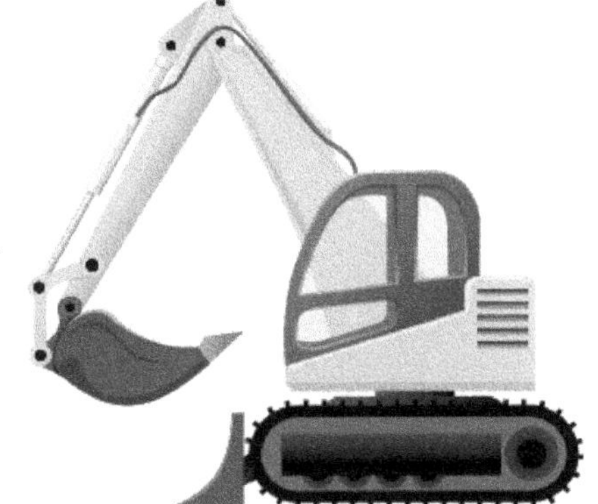

Before beginning mechanical excavation, archaeologists will use various mapping techniques to create an accurate map of the area to be excavated. This map will include features such as the type of soil, topographic features, and any potential archaeological features. Once the area is mapped, archaeologists will then create a plan of action for the excavation process.

The mechanical excavation process may be divided into two phases:

I. The removal of the topsoil and the excavation of the archaeological features. During the topsoil removal phase, the machine will remove the topsoil down to the archaeological layer. During this phase, the archaeological team will collect any artifacts that may be found in the topsoil.

II. Once the topsoil has been removed, archaeologists will begin the excavation of the archaeological features. During this phase, the machine will remove the soil in a controlled manner, allowing the archaeological team to identify and collect any artifacts or features that may be found.

III. Once the archaeological features have been excavated, the archaeological team will begin the process of cleaning, sorting, and analyzing the artifacts and features that were found. This process can involve the use of various techniques such as radiocarbon dating, DNA analysis, and soil sampling.

Mechanical excavation is a useful tool in archaeology that allows archaeologists to gain greater access to deeper archaeological deposits and to speed up the excavation process. It is a process that requires careful planning and execution in order to ensure that archaeological artifacts and features are carefully collected and analysed.

8. SCREENING EXCAVATION

Screening excavation is a process used in archaeology to separate and identify artifacts, or small pieces of material culture, such as coins, pottery, and bones, from the soil of an archaeological site. The process of screening archaeological material is a labour-intensive and time-consuming process, but is critical to the recovery and analysis of artifacts, as it allows archaeologists to identify and collect artifacts that may otherwise go unnoticed in the soil.

I. The process of screening excavation begins with the selection and preparation of a screening surface. This surface may be made of wood, metal, or plastic, and is typically a grid-like pattern that allows for the sorting and recording of artifacts.

The screening surface should be large enough to accommodate the amount of material that will be processed from the excavation site.

II. After the screening surface is prepared, archaeologists will begin to screen the material from the excavation. This process can involve the use of mechanical sieves, which are designed to separate larger pieces of material from the soil, or the use of manual methods, such as hand-sorting or flotation.

Mechanical sieves can be used to separate larger artifacts, such as stone tools, or to process bulk soil samples to retrieve smaller artifacts, such as pottery sherds. Manual methods, such as hand-sorting, are typically used to process smaller artifacts, such as coins, or to search for material that is too small to be detected through the use of sieves.

III.   When screening artifacts, archaeologists will look for any visible signs of cultural material, such as pottery sherds, coins, or stone tools. Artifacts that are recovered are carefully recorded, catalogued, and stored for further analysis.

This recording process is essential for archaeological research, as it provides a record of the artifacts and their context within the site.

Screening excavation is a critical process for archaeological research, as it allows archaeologists to retrieve and analyze artifacts from an excavation site. Through the use of mechanical sieves, hand-sorting, and flotation, archaeologists are able to identify, record, and analyze artifacts from an excavation site, providing valuable information about the past.

9. HORIZONTAL EXCAVATION

Horizontal excavation is a technique used in archaeology for uncovering the archaeological remains of a site. It is the most common form of excavation used in the field and involves the removal of layers of soil or other materials in order to uncover artifacts, features, and other remains of past human activity. The goal of horizontal

excavation is to identify and document the archaeological record of a site.

I. The process of horizontal excavation begins with the selection of an excavation unit or "area of interest." This is an area of the site that will be excavated and studied in detail.

The size of the unit is determined by the goals of the excavation, the size of the site, and the tools available.

II. Once the unit has been selected, the excavators prepare the site by clearing vegetation and marking the boundaries of the unit.
III. Next, the excavators begin to remove the layers of soil or other materials in the unit. This is usually done using hand tools such as trowels, shovels, and hoes. The layers are removed one at a time in order to preserve the archaeological record.
IV. As the layers are removed, the archaeologist carefully records the artifacts, features, and other remains that are uncovered.
V. Once the unit has been completely excavated, the archaeologist can begin the analysis of the artifacts, features, and other remains. This analysis is used to determine the date and nature of the site, as well as its cultural and historical context.
VI. The results of the analysis are documented in a report, which is then used to interpret the site and its significance.

Horizontal excavation is a vital part of archaeological research. It is a precise and systematic method of uncovering the archaeological record of a site. It allows archaeologists to document the artefacts, features, and other remains that are found, which provides valuable insights into the past.

10. Vertical Excavation

Vertical excavation is a technique used in archaeology to uncover and record archaeological sites. It is a process of systematically digging and exposing archaeological deposits, as well as the structural elements associated with them, from the surface to the deepest point of archaeological interest. This approach is commonly used when a site is too large to be excavated in a horizontal manner.

I. The first step in vertical excavation is to establish a grid system. This is done by placing markers in the ground at regular intervals and then stretching strings between them. This creates a set of reference points that allow the archaeologists to measure and map the site.

II. Once the grid is established, the archaeologists begin to dig in a vertical manner, exposing the archaeological deposits and features.

III. As the archaeologists dig, they will carefully remove the soil in layers, often using trowels and other small tools.

IV. Each layer is then carefully examined and mapped. The archaeologists will often take photographs of each layer in order to better document the site. They may also take samples of the soil for further analysis.

V. Once the archaeologists have reached the deepest point of archaeological interest, they will begin the process of backfilling. This is done by carefully refilling the excavated area with the soil that was removed, layer by layer.

VI.   As each layer is backfilled, the archaeologists will often take samples or photographs of the area in order to better record the site.

Vertical excavation is an important part of archaeological research. It allows archaeologists to uncover and document large sites, as well as to better understand the history and development of a particular area.

11. SHOVEL TESTING

Shovel testing is a common archaeological method used to survey an area for archaeological remains. This process involves digging a series of small, shallow pits, typically about 50-60cm deep, spaced approximately 2-3 metres apart. Shovel testing is typically done in areas where archaeological remains are suspected to be present, such as near ancient settlements, or in areas of known archaeological interest.

I.   The shovel test pits are usually dug by hand, although in some cases they may be dug using mechanical equipment. The pits are dug in a systematic way, usually in a grid pattern, to ensure that the entire area is tested thoroughly.

II.   The soil is then sifted and examined for any artifacts or features. Artifacts and features are identified, recorded, and sometimes collected and catalogued for further study.

Shovel testing is an important part of archaeological research, as it can provide valuable information about the area and its past inhabitants. The artifacts found can also help to establish a timeline of activity in the area.

Shovel testing is often used in combination with other methods, such as metal detection and aerial photography. The combination of these methods helps to create an overall picture of the site and its history.

12. BULK EXCAVATION

Bulk excavation is a form of archaeological excavation that involves the removal of large volumes of soil from a given area. It is used to uncover archaeological sites, artifacts, and other features that may be buried beneath the surface. Bulk excavation can be a time-consuming process, especially if the archaeological site is large. Archaeologists typically use a variety of tools, including shovels, picks, and trowels, to remove soil and other materials from the site.

I. Before beginning the process of bulk excavation, archaeologists must first identify the target area. This is usually done by conducting a preliminary survey of the site.

The survey may involve using aerial photography, ground-penetrating radar, or other remote sensing technologies to locate archaeological features that are buried beneath the surface.

II. Once the target area is identified, archaeologists can begin to plan the bulk excavation process.

Archaeologists typically divide the target area into sections, or "units."

III. Each unit is then excavated in a systematic manner, beginning with the removal of the topsoil. This soil is set aside for further analysis and study.

IV. Archaeologists then begin to remove soil in layers, or "strata." Each layer is carefully examined for artifacts and other features that may be present. Artifacts and features are then mapped, photographed, and studied.

V. Once the excavation of a particular layer is complete, archaeologists will often backfill the area with soil or other materials before moving on to the next layer.

VI. This helps to preserve the archaeological features that have been uncovered and allows for any future archaeological work that may need to be done.

By carefully removing soil in layers, archaeologists can uncover and study important archaeological features that may otherwise remain hidden beneath the surface.

13. FLOTATION

Flotation is a process used in archaeology to recover small artifacts and plant remains from soil samples. It is a useful technique for recovering items that are too small or delicate to be picked up by hand. The process works by combining the soil sample with water and then mixing it in a tank. As the mixture is stirred, air bubbles attach to the small artifacts, causing them to float to the surface. The artifacts can then be skimmed off the surface and collected.

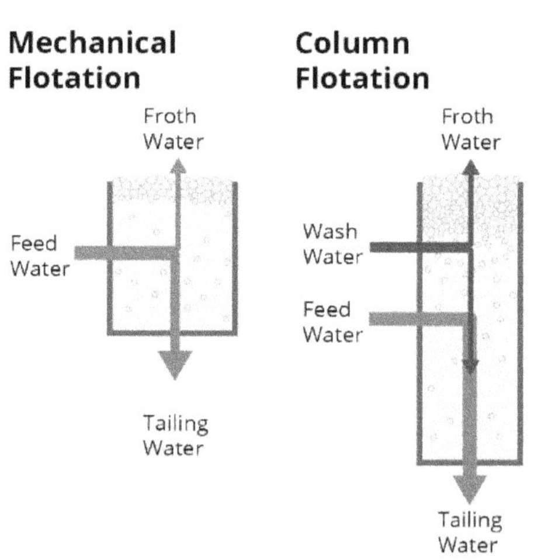

The process of flotation was developed in the early 20th century and was first used in mining to separate minerals from soil. In archaeology, the process has been used since the 1950s and has become a key part of archaeological investigations. Flotation makes it possible to recover small artifacts that would otherwise be missed, such as seeds, bones, and pottery fragments.

I.   To begin the process of flotation, soil samples are collected from an archaeological site.

II.   The soil is then sieved to remove any large artifacts that could interfere with the flotation process.

III.   The sieved soil is then placed in a container, such as a plastic bucket, and water is added.

IV.   The mixture is then stirred vigorously with a paddle or spoon to encourage the formation of bubbles.

V.   As the bubbles form, small artifacts are attached to them and rise to the surface.

VI.   Once the flotation process is complete, the artifacts can be skimmed off the surface and collected.

VII.   The artifacts are then sorted and analysed to gain insight into the archaeological site. Plant remains are often identified and analysed to gain information about the environment and diet of past peoples.

In addition to the collection of artifacts, flotation can also be used to recover pollen, which can provide valuable information about the environment at the time of the archaeological investigation. Pollen analysis can be used to determine the vegetation of the area and the climate, which can then be used to interpret the archaeological site.

14. Dry Sieving Or Water Sieving

Dry sieving or water sieving is a process used in archaeology to separate small artifacts from the soil. The process involves passing soil through a sieve, made up of a mesh of metal or plastic that is of a certain size. This allows the smaller artifacts to pass through the mesh, while the larger particles are retained, making it easier to find and collect the artifacts.

The process of dry sieving is relatively simple and can be done by hand or with the help of a mechanical sieve.

- In **hand sieving**, a pile of soil is placed on top of the sieve and then shaken or stirred with a stick or some other tool to force the soil through the mesh.
- In **mechanical sieving**, the material is placed in a sieve machine which uses a rotating drum to force the material through the mesh.

Water sieving is a process that uses water to separate small artifacts from the soil.

- In this process, the soil is placed in a container filled with water and agitated to allow the heavier particles to settle on the bottom. The lighter particles, including artifacts, then float to the top, where they can be collected. The size of the mesh used in the sieving process is important, as it determines what type of artifacts can be found.
- Generally, a mesh size of 2.0 to 2.5 mm is used for dry sieving, while a mesh size of 1.0 to 1.5 mm is used for water sieving. This allows for the smaller artifacts to pass through the mesh while the larger particles are retained.

The sieving process is an important part of archaeological research and can be used to find artifacts in a wide range of soil types. This process is especially useful in soils that have been disturbed by digging or other activities, as it can help to locate artifacts that may have been missed by traditional archaeological methods.

In addition to helping to locate artifacts, the sieving process can also be used to clean and sort artifacts. In this process, artifacts can be sorted by size, shape, and material, which can help to determine the age and origin of the artifacts.

15. PROBING

Probing in archaeology is a method of archaeological excavation used to identify the presence of archaeological features and artifacts below the ground surface. It involves inserting a long, pointed metal rod into the ground to make  small holes in the soil, and then retrieving the items that are found. In some cases, a variety of tools are used to probe the ground, such as a trowel, pick, or mattock.

I.   The first step in probing is to determine the exact location of the area to be probed. This is done by using a map, a GPS unit, or other surveying equipment to mark the area.

Once the area has been marked, excavation can begin.

II.   The next step is to remove the topsoil from the area to be probed. This is done by hand or with a shovel or other tools. The topsoil is cleared away to expose the underlying soil.

III.   Once the area is cleared, the archaeologist will begin to insert the metal rod into the ground. The rod is inserted several inches into the soil, and then withdrawn to see what artifacts or features have been uncovered.

IV.   If anything is found, it is carefully marked and recorded for further study.

V.   The archaeologist will then move to a new area and repeat the process.

VI.   This process is repeated until the entire area has been probed.

Probing can be used to identify artifacts and features that may not be visible on the surface, such as walls, structures, and graves. It can also be used to identify buried artifacts, such as pottery shards, tools, and coins.

16. PIT AND DUMP

Pits and dumps are two common features found in an archaeological excavation.

A pit is an archaeological feature that is a man-made, usually shallow, excavation in the ground. Pits are used to store artifacts and other materials, as well as to bury and discard them.

A dump is a man-made feature that is created when an archaeological site is disturbed and material is deposited in a pile. Dumps are commonly found in the form of middens, which are piles of discarded shells, bones, and other materials.

Analysis (Or Post-Excavation Analysis)

Post excavation analysis in archaeology is the process of examining, interpreting and reconstructing the material remains of a past human culture. It involves the collection, assessment, and analysis of artifacts, features and other archaeological data in order to gain an understanding of past human life and activity. Post excavation analysis is a crucial part of the archaeological process as it helps to create a more complete picture of past societies and their activities.

Post excavation analysis is a multi-faceted and complex process that involves a variety of different techniques and approaches. It begins with the collection and organization of artifacts and other archaeological data, followed by the analysis of the data to gain an understanding of how the artifacts and other data were used in the past. This analysis can include the study of wear patterns on artifacts, the examination of chemical composition, the examination of spatial patterns, and the comparison of artifacts between sites. The analysis of artifacts, features, and other archaeological data is often supplemented by the study of other historical records such as written texts, paintings, and photographs.

Various Methods And Their Processes

A. Inorganic Remains

Inorganic remains are artifacts and features that are made from materials that are not derived from living organisms. Inorganic remains are typically found in an archaeological context and can include manufactured items like pottery, tools and weapons, and building materials. They can also include geological features such as stone quarries, rock art, and river beds. Inorganic remains are important for understanding the activities of ancient peoples as well as the environmental conditions in which they lived.

Inorganic remains provide evidence of the materials and technologies used by ancient cultures. For example, pottery can provide information on the type of clay used, the shape of the vessel, and any decorations. This can help archaeologists identify a specific culture and the time period when the pottery was made. Inorganic remains can also provide evidence of a culture's trade networks, as artifacts may be imported from other areas. In addition, inorganic remains can provide evidence of the environment in which a culture lived, such as river beds that may indicate the presence of a river in the past.

1. POTTERY STUDIES (OR POTTERY ANALYSIS)

Pottery analysis is a type of archaeological analysis used to determine the origin and date of pottery artifacts. This method of analysis is important in understanding the past and can provide a wealth of information about the culture and history of an area.

I.   The first step in pottery analysis is the examination of the artifact. This involves looking at the surface and shape of the pottery, as well as noting any decorations or markings that may be present. It is also important to note the size and weight of the pottery, as this can provide further information about the purpose of the artifact.

II. The next step in pottery analysis is to examine the chemical composition of the artifact. This is done by taking a sample of the pottery and testing it in a laboratory. Through testing, the type of clay used to make the pottery can be identified, as well as any other materials that may have been used in its construction, such as stones, shells, or other organic materials.

III. Once the chemical composition of the pottery has been determined, it is possible to determine the origin of the artifact. This is done by comparing the chemical composition of the artifact to that of known pottery from the same area or period.

IV. The last step in pottery analysis is to date the artifact. This is done by examining the chemical composition of the pottery and comparing it to other artifacts from the same period. By doing this, it is possible to determine the approximate date of manufacture.

Pottery analysis is an important part of archaeological research and can provide a wealth of information about the past. By examining the surface, shape, and chemical composition of pottery artifacts, it is possible to determine the origin and date of the artifact, as well as other information such as the type of clay used in its construction. This type of analysis can be a useful tool in understanding the history of an area and its culture.

2. STONE-TOOLS ANALYSIS

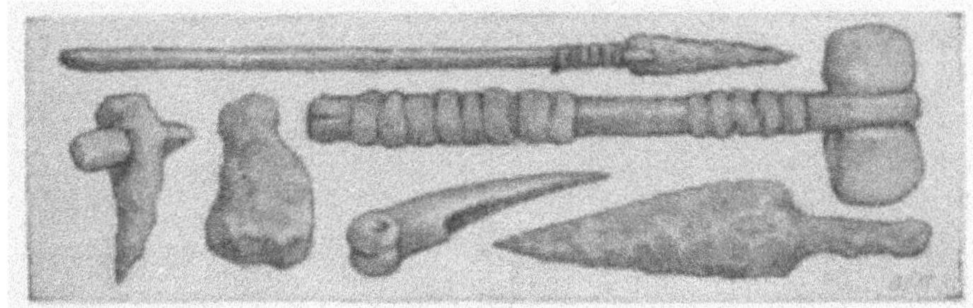

Stone tools analysis is a fundamental element of archaeological research. It encompasses a range of techniques that are used to identify, date, and interpret stone tools in an archaeological context.

I.   One of the first steps in the stone tools analysis process is the identification of the material used to make the artifact. The most common materials used in stone tools are chert, flint, obsidian, and quartzite.

Identification of the type of stone is important as it can provide information about availability and the potential sources of the material.

II.   Once the material has been identified, the stone tool is examined in order to identify its typology.

Typology is the categorization of stone tools based on the shape, size, and other characteristics. This is an important step in the analysis of stone tools as it provides an indication of the tool's function and the culture that produced it.

III.   The next step in the analysis is to determine how the artifact was made. This involves looking at the marks left on the artifact by the tool used to create it.

IV.   The final step in the analysis is to consider the context in which the artifact was found. This includes looking at where the artifact was discovered, what other artifacts were found nearby, and any other evidence that can be used to provide more information about the artifact and its use.

The analysis of stone tools is an important element of archaeological research as it provides invaluable insight into past societies and their technological, social, and economic practices.

3. METALLURGICAL ANALYSIS

Metallurgical analysis is an archaeological tool that helps archaeologists determine the composition of metal artifacts. It is the study of the physical and chemical properties of metal in order to determine the type of metal, its source, and its age.

Metallurgical analysis is used to identify the age, composition, and condition of metal artifacts, as well as to compare artifacts with other artifacts of similar origin.

I.   Metallurgical analysis typically begins with a visual observation of the artifact.
II.   This is followed by a physical examination of the object, which includes measuring its thickness, weight, and dimensions.
III.   The object is then cleaned and any corrosion or other damage is noted.
IV.   The next step in the process is a chemical analysis, which is conducted using a variety of techniques.

These techniques include x-ray fluorescence spectroscopy, x-ray diffraction, and electron microscopy. X-ray fluorescence spectroscopy is used to measure the elemental composition of the metal.

X-ray diffraction is used to identify the crystal structure of the metal, and electron microscopy is used to determine the grain size and shape of the metal.

V.   The next step is a macroscopic analysis of the artifact, which involves examining the object for signs of wear and tear, corrosion, and patination.

This helps to identify how the object was used and how it has aged.

VI.   Finally, the artifact is analysed using a range of techniques to determine its age. This includes analyzing the surface of the object, as well as any organic material that may be present on or around the object.

Radiocarbon dating and other methods of dating can be used to help determine the age of the artifact.

Metallurgical analysis is a useful tool for archaeologists, as it can provide valuable information about the composition of metal artifacts. It can help to identify the source of the metal, its age, and the type of metal used to make the artifact. It can also provide insight into how the object was used and how it has aged over time.

B. ORGANIC REMAINS

Organic remains in archaeology are materials that have been preserved due to their natural chemistry. These materials may include bones, wood, pollen, plants, and other remains that are often associated with human activity. Organic remains are an important source of information for archaeologists. They can provide evidence of ancient diets, trade, and subsistence patterns.

Organic remains can also provide insights into the environment and climate of a region at a given time. Organic remains may also be used to reconstruct past technologies and the way people interacted with their environment. By analysing the chemical composition of the remains, archaeologists can identify the species of plants, animals, and other organisms that were once present in a given area.

1. HUMAN REMAINS ANALYSIS

Human remains analysis in archaeology is the process of examining human skeletal remains to gain insight into life in the past. It includes studying the biological, social, and cultural aspects of an individual or a population. This type of analysis is often used to reconstruct the diet, activity patterns, and health of a past population, as well as to gain a better  understanding of their cultural beliefs and practices.

I. The first step of human remains analysis is to identify the remains as belonging to a particular individual or group.

This is done by analysing the morphology of the bone and comparing it to other known skeletal remains. This can help to determine the sex, age, and stature of the individual.

Other methods such as radiocarbon dating and DNA analysis can also be used to help establish the identity of the remains.

II. Once the identity of the remains has been established, the next step is to analyze the health and lifestyle of the individual or group.

This is done by examining the skeleton for any signs of trauma, disease, or nutritional deficiencies.

III. From this information, archaeologists can begin to reconstruct the diet, activity patterns, and health of a past population. For example, the presence of certain diseases or nutritional deficiencies can help to determine what types of food were available in the area. The wear and tear on the bones can be used to infer the types of labour and activities that the individual or population engaged in.

Faunal analysis is one of the most important tools used by archaeologists to reconstruct past environments, economies, and cultural practices. It involves the identification and analysis of animal remains recovered from archaeological sites.

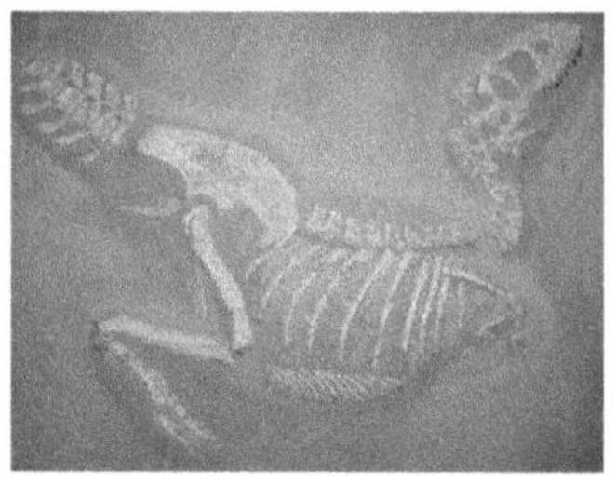

Faunal analysis can provide information about animals that were used for food, clothing, tools, and other materials. It can also provide insight into the human-animal relationship, which is of particular interest to many archaeologists.

I. The process of faunal analysis begins with the collection of animal remains from an archaeological site.

These remains are usually found in association with other artifacts and features and can include bones, teeth, antlers, horns, and shells.

II. The remains are then subjected to a series of analyses, including morphological, osteometric, and taphonomic.

Morphological analysis is the identification and description of the animal remains based on their size, shape, and other features.

Osteometric analysis is the measurement of the bones and teeth to determine the sex and age of the animal.

Taphonomic analysis looks at how the animal remains were changed over time due to natural processes, such as weathering and scavenging.

III.   Once the animal remains have been identified and analysed, they are then compared to modern specimens in order to determine their species and age.

This comparison can provide information about the diet of the people who lived at the site and the environment in which they lived. It can also provide information about the type of animal husbandry practices that were used.

IV.   The next step in faunal analysis is to interpret the data. This involves looking at patterns in the animal remains in order to gain an understanding of the site's cultural, economic, and environmental context. For example, an analysis of the animal bones from a hunter-gatherer site might reveal that the people hunted a wide variety of animals, which indicates that they had access to a variety of resources.

An analysis of the animal bones from an agricultural site might reveal that the people relied heavily on domesticated animals, which indicates that they had a more structured and intensive form of animal husbandry.

V.   Finally, the results of the faunal analysis are used to draw conclusions about the past. For example, the analysis of animal bones from a site can provide information about the environment that people lived in, the type of subsistence strategies they used, and the types of animals they used for food and other materials.

3. MOLLUSCS/INVERTEBRATE ANALYSIS

Mollusc or invertebrate analysis is a method of archaeological research that focuses on the study of small organisms, such as molluscs and other invertebrates, in order to gain insight into the past. This type of analysis can provide a wealth of information about the environment and climate of an archaeological site, as well as the activities of the people who lived there.

I. Mollusc and invertebrate analysis begin with the collection of specimens from an archaeological site. This can be done using a variety of methods, such as sieving, flotation, or hand collection.

II. Once the specimens have been collected, they are then identified and sorted into taxonomic categories. This allows archaeologists to determine the species composition of the site, which can provide information about the environment and climate of the area.

III. Once the specimens have been identified and sorted, they are then examined in more detail. This includes a close examination of the shells, which can provide information about the age and condition of the organism, as well as the diet and habitat of the species.

The shells can also be used to determine the age of the site, as certain species of molluscs and other invertebrates have distinct growth and mortality patterns that can be used to date sites.

In addition to examining the shells, archaeologists also analyze the archaeological context of the molluscs and invertebrates. This includes analyzing the faunal remains to determine the types of activities that were taking place at the site. For example, if a large number of molluscs are found among the remains, it could suggest that the site was a fishing ground. The analysis of the context can also provide information about the diet and lifestyle of the people who lived at the site.

IV.   Finally, archaeologists use the data they have gathered to reconstruct the environment and climate of the site. This can include reconstructing the type of environment in which the species lived, as well as the types of activities that took place around the site.

V.   This information can then be used to gain a better understanding of the past, including the history of the people who lived at the site.

4. BOTANICAL ANALYSIS

Botanical analysis is a type of archaeology that uses plant remains to gain further understanding of archaeological sites and the people who have lived there. This type of analysis allows archaeologists to understand what plants were growing in the area,  what they were used for, and how they may have been harvested. It is also used to determine if a site has been occupied or not, and to track changes in the environment over time.

I.   The first step in a botanical analysis is the collection and identification of the plant remains. Archaeologists may collect plant remains either directly from the site or from nearby areas.

II.   Once collected, the plant remains are identified and classified according to their type. This step helps to determine what kinds of plants were present at the site, and how they were distributed.

III.   Once the plant remains have been identified, archaeologists can begin to analyze them. This analysis can include a variety of methods, such as pollen analysis, seed analysis, phytolith analysis, and macro-botanical analysis.

Pollen analysis is used to identify the types of plants that were present at the site, as well as to track changes in the environment over time.

Seed analysis is used to determine how the plants were used, such as for food or medicine, and to identify the species of plants that were present.

Phytolith analysis looks at the microscopic remains of plants, such as the silica skeletons of grasses, and can help to identify the types of plants that were present.

Macro-botanical analysis looks at the larger remains of plants, such as the nuts, fruits, and grains, and can help to identify the types of plants that were grown and harvested.

IV.   Once the analysis of the plant remains is complete, archaeologists can begin to draw conclusions about the site and the people who lived there. They can determine what plants were growing in the area, what they were used for, and how they may have been harvested. They can also track changes in the environment over time, and make comparisons between different archaeological sites.

By collecting and analysing plant remains, archaeologists can gain insights into the lives of the people who have lived on a site and make comparisons with other sites. This type of analysis can help to understand the environment of the past, and how it has changed over time.

5. SEDIMENT ANALYSIS

Sediment analysis is an important tool used in archaeology to help understand the depositional history of a site. By studying the sediment deposits found in archaeological sites, archaeologists can gain important insights into the past environment, land use and other aspects of the cultural history of the site.

I. Sediment analysis begins with the collection of samples from the archaeological site. Samples are typically collected with a shovel or trowel in order to ensure that the sediment is undisturbed.

II. Once the samples are collected, they are placed in plastic bags and labelled with the site and location from which they were collected.

III. The next step in the sediment analysis process is to analyze the sediment samples in the laboratory. This involves a process called sieving, which separates the sediment into different size fractions.

The sieving process is important as it allows archaeologists to identify any artifacts, such as stone tools, pottery fragments, or bones, that may be present in the sediment.

IV. Once the different size fractions of sediment have been identified, they can be analysed further. This involves looking at the physical and chemical characteristics of the sediment, such as its grain size, colour, and composition.

Sediment analysis can also be used to identify the presence of pollen and other organic materials, as well as to determine the age of the sediment.

V. Finally, the results of the sediment analysis are used to interpret the depositional history of the site. This includes understanding the environment in which the sediment was deposited and how it has changed over time.

By studying the sediment and the artifacts found within it, archaeologists can gain important insights into the past environment, land use and other aspects of the cultural history of the site.

INTERPRETATION

Interpretation in archaeology is the process of constructing meaning from the evidence found at archaeological sites. It is a key part of the archaeological process and involves using evidence from the past to develop an understanding of the people and societies who lived there.

Archaeologists use a variety of methods to interpret the data they have gathered, including excavation, analysis of artefacts and other material remains, and historical and ethnographic research.

Archaeologists use a range of methods to interpret the data they have gathered, including historical and ethnographic research, which involves looking at written records and other sources of information about the people and societies who lived at the site.

Archaeologists also use a range of theoretical approaches to interpret the data they have gathered, such as environmental archaeology and post-processualism.

Ethnographic Interpretation: This type of interpretation looks at the living cultures of modern-day people to gain insight into the past.

Contextual Analysis is the study of the relationship between archaeological artefacts and their surrounding environment, such as the landscape or the local environment.

Environmental Reconstruction is the science of reconstructing ancient environments based on the available archaeological evidence. This type of interpretation can provide an insight into the environment and climate of the past.

Typological analysis is a method of archaeological classification that involves grouping artefacts and other remains based on shared characteristics. It is used to identify patterns in the archaeological record and can also provide insight into cultural development and behaviour.

Comparative analysis in archaeology is an established method of interpreting past human behaviour, by comparing and contrasting artifacts from different archaeological sites.

Conservation And Preservation

Conservation and preservation in archaeology are two distinct, yet related concepts.

Conservation is the process of caring for, repairing, and maintaining archaeological materials for long-term use and analysis.

Preservation refers to the process of protecting archaeological sites from damage, destruction, and vandalism, as well as from natural processes, such as erosion and weathering.

Both conservation and preservation are important for a variety of reasons, but the two terms should not be used interchangeably.

Process Of Conservation

I. The first step in the conservation process is to identify and assess the archaeological sites and artifacts that need to be conserved. Archaeologists will examine the artifacts, sites, and landscapes that need to be preserved, and assess the level of damage or destruction that has already occurred.

The assessment will help to determine the overall condition of the artifacts and sites, and the best methods for preserving them.

II. Once the artifacts and sites have been identified, the next step in the conservation process is to create a plan for their conservation. This plan will include the steps that need to be taken to protect the artifacts and sites from further damage or destruction.

It may include the use of protective materials, such as plaster or protective coatings, or the implementation of protective measures, such as fencing or barriers. It may also include the use of conservation techniques, such as stabilizing, cleaning, restoring, or preserving the artifacts or sites.

III. The third step in the conservation process is the implementation of the conservation plan. This may involve the use of protective materials or measures, as well as the use of conservation techniques.

It is important to ensure that the conservation techniques are done properly, as they can have a significant effect on the integrity of the artifacts and sites.

IV. Finally, the fourth step in the conservation process is to monitor the artifacts and sites to ensure that they remain in their original condition. This may involve periodic inspections of the artifacts and sites, as well as regular maintenance of protective materials or measures.

This monitoring is important as it helps to ensure that the artifacts and sites remain in their original condition and are not subjected to further damage or destruction.

PROCESS OF PRESERVATION

I. The first step in preservation is the identification and recording of archaeological sites.

This involves surveying the area to identify any artifacts or structures that may be present and recording their location, condition, and any other relevant information. This data can be used to make decisions about how best to protect the site and any artifacts.

II.   Once an archaeological site has been identified and recorded, it is important to protect it from damage.

This can be done by establishing buffer zones around the site and restricting access to it. This helps to preserve the physical characteristics of the site and prevent erosion or contamination from human activities.

It is also important to protect artifacts from damage. This involves cataloguing and storing artifacts in a secure, climate-controlled environment. This helps to preserve the artifacts and prevents them from deteriorating or becoming damaged.

Preservation also involves the conservation of artifacts. This involves cleaning and repairing artifacts, as well as stabilizing them with adhesives or consolidates. This helps to preserve their physical integrity and ensures that they remain in good condition.

III.   Finally, it is important to document archaeological sites and artifacts. This involves taking photographs, making drawings, and creating 3D models. This helps to create an accurate record of the site or artifact and provides a permanent record of its condition.

Public Outreach

Public outreach in archaeology is the use of education and communication activities to share archaeological discoveries and knowledge with the public. It is a form of public engagement that allows archaeologists to share their findings with the wider public. Public outreach in archaeology can help to promote the public's understanding of archaeological research and its importance in our understanding of the past.

Public outreach in archaeology can take many forms, including educational programming, public lectures, museum exhibitions, media appearances, educational websites and social media. Educational programming can include field trips, workshops and lectures that allow the public to learn more about archaeology and its methods. Public lectures provide an opportunity to discuss the significance of

archaeological discoveries, while museum exhibitions help to illustrate the importance of archaeological research and the past. Media appearances can also be used to reach a wider audience, as can educational websites and social media.

Public outreach in archaeology also involves engaging with the public in meaningful ways. Archaeologists can work with local communities to ensure that the public is involved in the process of archaeological research. This can include community archaeology projects wherein members of the public are invited to participate in archaeological activities, such as surveying and excavating. The public can also be invited to provide comments and opinions on research plans and proposals. The public's input can be used to ensure that research is conducted in an ethical manner.

Public outreach in archaeology can also involve working with local governments and other stakeholders. By engaging with these stakeholders, archaeologists 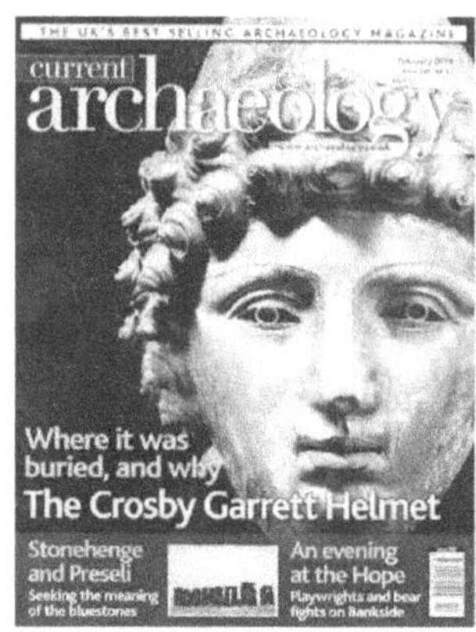

can ensure that archaeological research is conducted in a way that is beneficial to the community. This can include working with local governments to protect archaeological sites and ensure that they are not damaged by development or other activities. It can also include working with local communities to ensure that their traditional knowledge and cultural heritage is respected and preserved.

DATING

Dating in archaeology is the process of determining the age of a certain artifact or archaeological site. This is done through the analysis of artifacts or other materials found in the site, and comparing them to other materials from known time periods. Dating helps archaeologists determine the chronology and history of a site, as well as establish its importance.

KINDS OF DATING

A. RELATIVE DATING

1. TYPOLOGY

Study of different types of artifacts, such as pottery, tools, and other objects, in order to determine their age relative to each other. By studying the different types of artifacts and their associated dates, archaeologists are able to piece together a timeline of events that occurred in the past.

2. STRATIGRAPHY

Stratigraphy is a branch of geology that studies rock strata, or layers, in the Earth's crust. In relative dating, stratigraphy is used to determine the age of a fossil or artifact relative to other fossils or artifacts found in the same strata. Stratigraphy works by studying the age of layers of rock and the objects that are found within those layers.

3. SERIATION

Seriation, also known as artifact sequencing, is a technique used in relative dating to arrange artifacts in a chronological order based on their shape and style. By studying the physical characteristics of artifacts, archaeologists can determine the relative age of each item and develop a sequence of events for a particular site.

4. GEO-ARCHAEOLOGICAL DATING

Geo-archaeological dating, also known as geoarchaeology or archaeological geology, is a type of relative dating that uses geological and geomorphological features and regional context to determine the age and sequence of events in an archaeological site. This type of dating is typically used in sites that do not contain artifacts and can provide information about the environment in which the site was used. It is especially useful in sites where the absolute dating of materials is not possible.

5. OBSIDIAN HYDRATION DATING (OHD)

Obsidian Hydration Dating (OHD) is a relative dating technique used to date artifacts made from obsidian, a volcanic glass that formed from rapidly cooled lava. It is based on the fact that, over time, water slowly diffuses into the surface of the obsidian, leaving a visible hydration rind. By measuring the thickness of the hydration rind, scientists can calculate the amount of time that has passed since the obsidian was formed. This technique is most commonly used to date relatively young artifacts (less than 10,000 years old).

6. CHEMICAL DATING OF BONES

Chemical dating of bones in relative dating is a method of determining the age of fossils based on the relative concentrations of certain elements, such as uranium, within the fossil. This method can be used to determine the approximate age of a fossil, but not the exact age.

7. OPTICALLY STIMULATED LUMINESCENCE (OSL)

Optically Stimulated Luminescence (OSL) is a technique used in relative dating to determine the age of sediment deposits. It works by measuring the amount of light energy absorbed by quartz grains when they are exposed to light. This absorbed energy is stored in the grains and can be used to estimate the amount of time that has passed since the grains were last exposed to sunlight. The technique is particularly useful for dating sediment deposits in contexts such as archaeological sites and is often used in combination with other relative dating techniques.

8. FLUORINE TEST

Fluorine dating is a relative dating method that can be used to determine the relative age of a specimen by measuring the amount of fluorine absorbed from other materials in the same environment. The amount of fluorine absorbed indicates how long the specimen has been in the environment.

9. NITROGEN TEST

Nitrogen test is a relative dating technique that uses the amount of nitrogen absorbed by an organism to calculate its age. This method is used to date organic materials such as wood, charcoal, and fossils. It is based on the fact that the amount of nitrogen absorbed by an organism decreases over time, and the older the organism, the less nitrogen it contains. By measuring the amount of nitrogen in a sample, scientists can calculate the approximate age of the material.

10. POLLEN TEST

Pollen test in relative dating is a method of relative dating that relies on the analysis of the types of pollen found in a soil sample. By comparing the types of pollen found in different layers of sediment, scientists can determine the relative age of each layer. This information can then be used to reconstruct the environmental conditions and climate changes over time.

A. ABSOLUTE DATING

1. RADIO CARBON DATING [C-14]

Radio carbon dating is a method of absolute dating which uses the decay of carbon-14 to estimate the age of organic materials up to about 60,000 years old. It is based on the fact that carbon-14 is constantly being created in the atmosphere by cosmic rays, and then absorbed by plants and animals as part of their normal life cycle.

When an organism dies, it no longer absorbs new carbon-14, and the existing carbon-14 begins to decay at a known rate. By measuring the amount of carbon-14 remaining in the sample and calculating the time at which half of the carbon-14 would have decayed, scientists can estimate the age of the material.

2. DENDROCHRONOLOGY

Dendrochronology is a form of absolute dating which relies on the use of tree rings to determine the age of an object. It is one of the most precise forms of absolute dating and can be used to accurately determine the age of archaeological artifacts, living trees, and other organic materials.

3. THERMO-LUMINESCENCE

Thermo-luminescence is a method of absolute dating used in archaeology and other fields to determine the age of an object by measuring the amount of light emitted from the object when it is heated. It is based on the principle that minerals and other materials absorb energy from the surrounding environment, and when heated, they release some of this energy in the form of light. By measuring the amount of light emitted from an object, the age of the object can be determined.

4.   ARCHAEOMAGNETISM

Archaeomagnetism is a dating technique used to date archaeological materials based on their interaction with Earth's magnetic field. This technique relies on the fact that the Earth's magnetic field changes over time, and that archaeological materials, such as ceramics or bricks, cool and become magnetized in the direction of the magnetic field at the time of cooling. By measuring and comparing the current magnetic orientation of the archaeological materials to the known magnetic orientation in the past, archaeologists can accurately date materials up to several thousand years old.

5.   POTASSIUM-ARGON [K-AR] DATING

Potassium-argon dating is a form of absolute dating based on the rate of decay of the radioactive isotope potassium-40 into argon-40. This technique is useful for dating materials that are millions of years old. It is especially useful for materials from volcanic rocks as the argon released from the decay of potassium-40 is trapped in the crystalline structure of the volcanic material.

Common Tools Used In Archaeology

1. Directional Compass

- Directional compasses are commonly used in archaeology to help orient archaeological features and artifacts.
- Compasses are used to help locate features in the field, to measure and record directions in the field, and to map the location of features and artifacts in the laboratory.

- Compasses are also used to orient excavation trenches and map the area of excavation, as well as to orient structures in the field.

2. Global Positioning system (GPS) Machine

- GPS machines are used in archaeology to help locate sites, features, and artifacts in the field.
- GPS machines are used to accurately map the area of an archaeological site and to record the coordinates of features and artifacts in the field.
- GPS machines are also often used to help orient excavation trenches and to map the area of excavation.

3. LEVELLING MACHINE

- Levelling machines can be used to measure the earth's surface and establish horizontal and/or vertical datums for archaeological excavations.

- Levelling machines can be used to map the contours of the land surface, allowing archaeologists to detect any changes in the land surface over time.
- Levelling machines can be used to accurately measure the elevation of archaeological features, helping archaeologists to understand the relationship between different features and the environment.

4. CAMERA

- Camera can be used to document archaeological sites and artifacts in detail. By documenting artifacts in situ and in close-up, archaeologists are able to study, analyze, and interpret these artifacts in much greater detail than if they were relying on sketches or drawings.
- Camera can also be used to create 3D models of archaeological sites. By using multiple pictures, archaeologists can create 3D models of sites and artifacts. These models can help to visualize

how a site would have looked in the past, and can be used for further analysis and interpretation.

5. Measuring Tape

- Measuring Tape is used in archaeological excavations to map the layout of a site, measure distances between features, and track the relative depth of features.

- Measuring Tape is also used to accurately measure the dimensions of artifacts, features, and soil layers, as well as to take elevations of the site.

6. Pegging

- Pegging is a process used in archaeology to survey the context of a site. It involves marking the boundaries of a site or feature using metal or wooden pegs, which are then documented in a plan.
- Pegging is also used to mark the position of important features or objects within a site, such as artifacts, features, or structures. This information can then be used to help interpret the site and provide a better understanding of its history.

7. Spade

- **Digging:** Spades are used to dig into the ground to uncover artifacts and features in an archaeological site. It's a tool that every archaeologist must have.

• **Trowelling:** Spades can also be used to trowel away dirt and debris in order to uncover artifacts and features. This is often done in a more delicate manner than digging, as it allows the archaeologist to better identify the artifacts and features in the ground.

8. HAND PICK

- Hand picking is a technique used by archaeologists to carefully remove artifacts or features from a matrix without causing damage or destroying any associated context. This method is used when the context of the archaeological remains is of primary importance and the artifacts or features must be carefully removed from the area of excavation.
- Hand picking is especially beneficial when dealing with fragile artifacts and features, such as charred wood, pottery, and other small items. It is also useful for removing soil layers and deposits, as well as for excavating stratigraphic layers.

9. SHOVEL

- Shovels are used to remove large amounts of sediment or soil to expose archaeological features, such as walls, floors, and hearths.
- Shovels are also used to dig trial trenches to determine the age, type, and nature of archaeological deposits.

10. Soil Carrying Wheelbarrow, Baskets And Trays

- Soil carrying wheelbarrows, baskets and trays are used in archaeology to transport soil and other materials that need to be removed from an excavation site. This can include soil that has been dug up during a dig, as well as artifacts and other items that may have been found during the excavation.

- Wheelbarrows, baskets and trays are used to transport the soil and other items from the excavation area to a designated area where it can be more closely examined and studied. These tools are also used to transport soil and other materials between different excavation sites.

11. Soil Colour Chart

- Soil colour charts can be used to identify changes in the soil profile, which can indicate the presence of archaeological features, such as postholes and ditches.

- Soil colour charts can be used to determine the composition of archaeological deposits, such as ash, midden, and fill. This can provide important information about the different phases of occupation at a site.

12. TWINE

- Twine is used to measure and mark off areas in an archaeological site. It can be used to make a grid or to define boundaries for a particular area of excavation. 
- Twine is also used to tie artifacts to stakes or other markers in order to keep track of their exact location and to prevent them from being moved or disturbed.

13. DIRECTIONAL ARROW

- Directional arrow in archaeology is used to indicate the direction of movement of ancient people or to indicate the direction of the flow of a waterway.
- Directional arrow is also used to identify the location of an archaeological feature or a structure, such as a house, a temple, or a burial site.

14. SAMPLE BAG

- Sample Bags are used to store and transport artifacts and other items that have been collected during an archaeological excavation. These sample bags are typically numbered and labelled for easy identification.
- Sample Bags can also be used to separate different types of artifacts from each other in order to avoid cross-contamination. This is especially important when dealing with organic materials, such as wood and bone, which can be easily damaged or altered through contact with other materials.

15. FOIL PAPER

- Preservation of Organic Materials: Foil paper is used to wrap and preserve organic materials such as bone, wood, leather, and textiles. This helps to prevent them from deteriorating and allows for further analysis.
- Non-Destructive Archaeological Analysis: Foil paper can be used to cover artifacts during non-destructive analysis, such as X-ray fluorescence or radiocarbon dating, which can help to date artifacts or identify their chemical composition.

16. IDENTIFICATION TAG

- Identification tags can be used in archaeology to keep track of artifacts found during an excavation. The tags may contain the location, date, and description of the artifacts, as well as other relevant information. This helps to keep track of the artifacts and can provide scientists with valuable information about the site.
- Tagging Artifacts: Archaeologists may use identification tags to tag artifacts found during an excavation. Tagging an artifact is a way to identify it and record its location, date, and other relevant information. This helps scientists to keep track of the artifacts and can provide them with valuable information about the site.

17. DOCUMENTATION FORM

- Documentation forms provide the basic information needed to understand and interpret the archaeological record. They provide a way of recording the context and details of archaeological findings, and allow for the comparison and analysis of data from different sites.
- Documentation forms are also used to record information about the site itself, such as the topography and geology of

the area, and any cultural features present. This information can then be used to support research into the past and to inform future archaeological projects.

18. Graph Sheet

- Graph sheets are used to document the vertical and horizontal measurements at an archaeological site. This is often done to create a map of the site and help in the interpretation of the site.
- Graph sheets are also used to document the stratigraphy of an archaeological site. This helps archaeologists to understand the sequence of events that have occurred at the site, as well as the relationship between different layers of material.